Saxmania!
Great Solos.

Wise Publications
London/New York/Paris/Sydney/Copenhagen/Madrid

Exclusive Distributors:
Music Sales Limited
8/9 Frith Street,
London W1V 5TZ, England.
Music Sales Pty Limited
120 Rothschild Avenue,
Rosebery, NSW 2018,
Australia.

Order No. AM90123
ISBN 0-7119-3185-2
This book © Copyright 1993 by Wise Publications

Compiled by Peter Evans
Music arranged by Steve Tayton
Music processed by Ternary Graphics

Book design by Studio Twenty, London
Cover photograph by Julian Hawkins

Printed in the United Kingdom by
Halstan & Co Limited, Amersham, Buckinghamshire.

Your Guarantee of Quality
As publishers, we strive to produce every book
to the highest commercial standards.
The music has been freshly engraved and the book has been
carefully designed to minimise awkward page turns and to
make playing from it a real pleasure.
Particular care has been given to specifying acid-free,
neutral-sized paper which has not been elemental chlorine bleached
but produced with special regard for the environment.
Throughout, the printing and binding have been planned to ensure
a sturdy,attractive publication which should give years of enjoyment.
If your copy fails to meet our high standards, please
inform us and we will gladly replace it.

Music Sales' complete catalogue lists thousands of titles and is free from
your local music shop, or direct from Music Sales Limited.
Please send a cheque/postal order for £1.50 for postage to: Music Sales Limited,
Newmarket Road, Bury St. Edmunds, Suffolk IP33 3YB.

And just look at some of the other
music you can play with Saxmania!…

Saxmania! Standards
Includes 'Catch A Falling Star'…
'As Time Goes By'…'Pennies From Heaven'…
and 31 more golden favourites.
Order No.AM78262

Saxmania! Jazz Hits
Includes 'Mood Indigo'…
'Take The 'A' Train'…'Take Five'…
and two dozen more all-time greats.
Order No.AM78254

Saxmania! Pop Greats
Includes 'Sailing'…'Stand By Me'…
'Nothing's Gonna Change My Love For You'…
and 29 more chart hits.
Order No.AM78247

Saxmania! Jazz Classics
Includes 'On The Sunny Side Of The Street'…
'Walking Shoes'…'Cute'…and 30 other jazz classics.
Order No.AM90100

Saxmania! Rock Hits
Includes 'Addicted To Love'…'Layla'…'Roxanne'…
and 20 other rock classics.
Order No.AM90101

Saxmania! Blues Greats
Includes 'Basin Street Blues'…
'Georgia On My Mind'…'Lazy Bones'…
and over 30 other essential blues numbers.
Order No.AM90099

Saxmania! Beatles Classics
Includes 'Eleanor Rigby'…'Hey Jude'…
'Yesterday'…and 32 other famous Beatles hits.
Order No.N090462

Saxmania! Big Band
Includes 'A Taste Of Honey'…'Night Train'…
'Opus One'…and 33 other Big Band numbers.
Order No.AM90122

Aja

Words & Music by Walter Becker & Donald Fagen
Sax Solo by Wayne Shorter

The interplay between the rhythmic stabs by the rhythm section playing dominant chords, and the fluidly powerful saxophone over bars 1 to 10, builds tension, until a sense of release is achieved at bars 11 to 17. The build-up starts again at bar 18, with a slowly rising Mixolydian scale, releasing tension at bar 26 to a gentle end of solo.

N.B. A Mixolydian scale has semitones on the 3rd – 4th and 6th – 7th degrees of the scale.

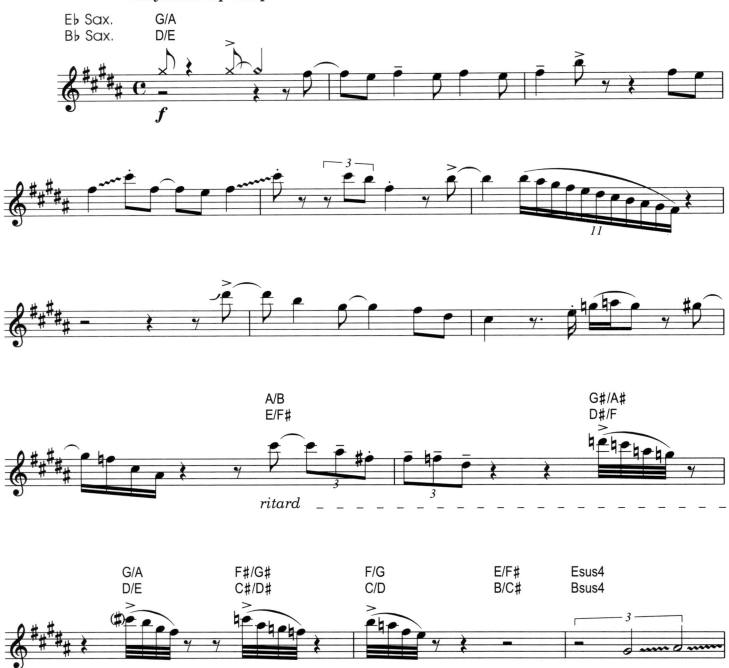

Baker Street

Words & Music by Gerry Rafferty
Sax Solo by Raphael Ravenscroft

A well known solo, which needs a lot of control of the reed for the opening glissando. Experiment by pitching the starting note D, then gradually opening the keys up, increasing tension on the reed, until you reach the top note.

Careless Whisper

Words & Music by George Michael & Andrew Ridgeley
Sax Solo by Steve Gregory

A fine example of good phrasing, breath control and legato playing of a strong, lyrical tune.

9

Fortress Around Your Heart

Words & Music by Sting
Sax Solo by Branford Marsalis

This is a modal solo based on a Dorian scale which has semitones on the 2nd – 3rd and 6th – 7th degrees of the scale. The pedal bass note (G concert) is the root and B♭ is inserted to keep the scale form. Rhythmic interjections, across the beat, maintain interest and give added spice.

* This vocal line is pitched for Saxophone and is intended as a vocal guide only.

Just The Two Of Us

Words & Music by Ralph MacDonald, William Salter & Bill Withers
Sax Solo by Grover Washington

The extremities of the saxophone are used here. For the lower notes, keep the lower jaw relaxed (say "Aaww" to open the throat) and keep pressure on the lower lip. Most of the solo is based on a pentatonic (i.e. five-note) scale.

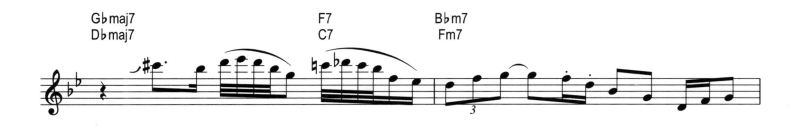

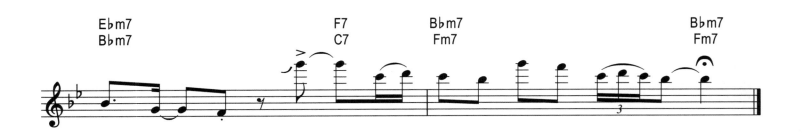

Lily Was Here

Music by David A. Stewart
Sax Solo by Candy Dulfer

Good example of trading phrases between guitar and saxophone, liberally sprinkled with pentatonic and blues scales, which fit all the chords in the tune.
N.B. Blues scale: minor 3rd – tone – semitone – semitone – minor 3rd – tone.

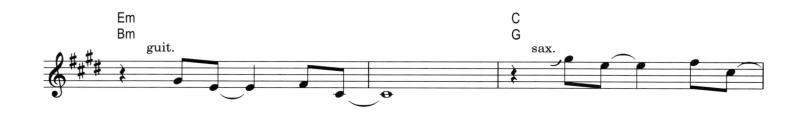

Pick Up The Pieces

Music by Roger Ball & Hamish Stuart
Sax Solo by Tom Scott

The solo is played an octave higher than written. You need good reed control for high harmonics –
as a preparation exercise, play a low B♭ or B, with the octave key depressed, and by varying the
lip pressure, try to play the harmonics. (It should sound like a bugle call.)

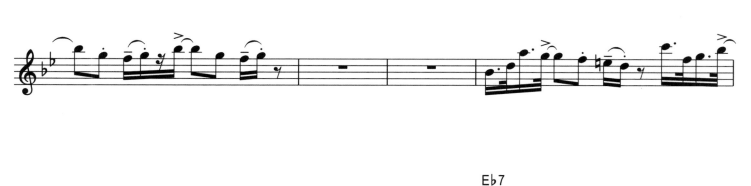

Eb7
Bb7

Eb7
Bb7

F7
C7

Bbm7
Fm7

1.

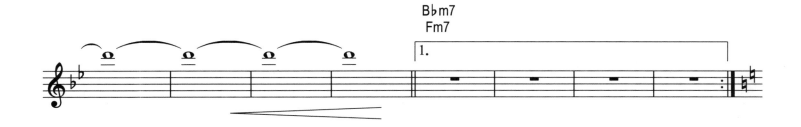

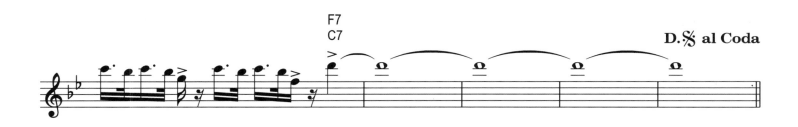

Redemption Song

Words & Music by Bob Marley
Sax Solo by Courtney Pine

This piece is relaxed and laid back in a Rubato style, which literally means "robbed time". Aim for a legato feel (smoothly connected).

Sister Moon

Words & Music by Sting
Sax Solo by Branford Marsalis

Exotic soprano playing. A great example of accompanying a vocal line. It is important to play in all keys, especially if the composer is a guitarist, since the tunes are usually written in a 'difficult' key for sax, i.e. E major becomes C♯ major on E♭ saxophones, or A major becomes B major on B♭ saxophones.

* *This vocal line is pitched for Saxophone and is intended as a vocal guide only.*

whole night through and they real-ly don't care if I do __ oo - oo I'd go

out of my __ mind but for you __ oo. _____

___ Sis - ter moon.

Slightly Out Of Tune (Desafinado)

English Lyrics by Jon Hendricks & Jessie Cavanaugh
Music by Antonio Carlos Jobim
Sax Solo by Stan Getz

The best sort of vibrato on a saxophone is generally accepted as being the jaw method. The success of this is dependent on the position of the jaw, a relaxed throat and good lip support. Blow a note and say "ah-ah-ah-ah" in groups of four, moving the jaw up and down slightly.

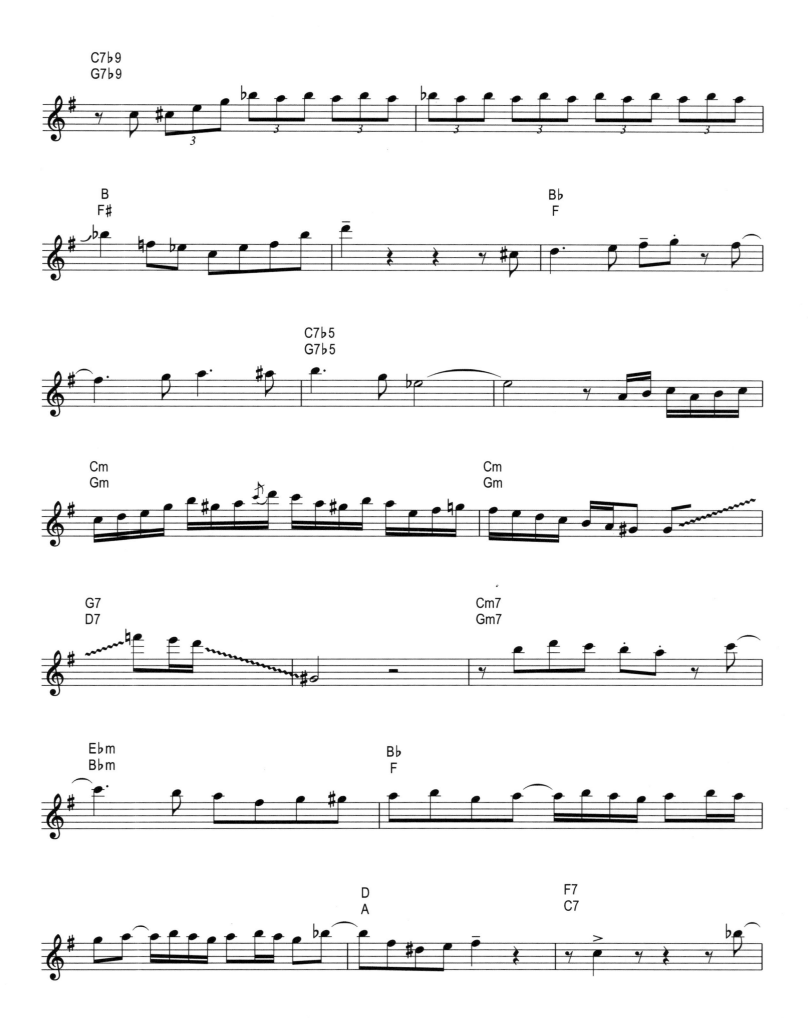

Songbird

Music by Kenny G.
Sax Solo by Kenny G.

This tune is based around a pentatonic scale, and gets progressively more difficult to play.

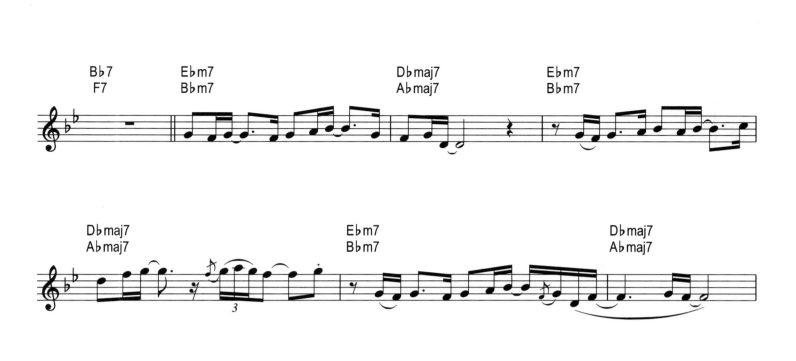

42

43

Starsky & Hutch

Music by Tom Scott
Sax Solo by Tom Scott

Hard driving tenor playing. Usually players who achieve this level of projection are using a mouthpiece with a long facing and fairly wide tip opening, with a medium soft to hard reed, depending on the strength of the facial muscles. This is something intermediate players should build up to, using softer reeds and clipping them a little to make them harder if necessary.

Your Latest Trick

Words & Music by Mark Knopfler
Sax Solo by Michael Brecker

This piece should be played with a full tone. Make sure you have a good mouthpiece and reed, and above all a good instrument; (all the best players do!). Pay particular attention to the lip slurs, grace notes and glissandi.

All the mid-night bar-gains have been struck

* *This vocal line is pitched for Saxophone and is intended as a vocal guide only.*

be-tween the sa - tin beaus and their belles.

Pre-his-to - ric gar-bage - trucks have the ci-ty to them - selves.

Ech-oes roar din - o-saurs they're all do-in' the mon - ster ma - sh, and

most of the ta-xis, most of the whores are on-ly tak-ing calls for cash,___ m - mm ___

I don't know how it hap-pened, it all took place so quick, but

all I can do is hand it to you ___ and your la-test trick.

7/00 (37547)